14.95

WITH

3 1192 00594 5090

N

THE SECRET LANGUAGE

THE SECRET LANGUAGE

PHEROMONES IN THE ANIMAL WORLD

Rebecca L. Johnson

Lerner Publications Company • Minneapolis

To my best friend, Leland, for his
unending support and encouragement

Library of Congress Cataloging-in-Publication Data

Johnson, Rebecca L.
      The secret language: pheromones in the animal world / by Rebecca
    L. Johnson
        p.   cm.
      Includes index.
      Summary: Examines how some animals communicate through the
    chemicals known as pheromones.
      ISBN 0-8225-1586-5 (lib. bdg.)
      1. Animal communication—Juvenile literature. 2. Pheromones—
    Juvenile literature. [1. Pheromones. 2. Animal communication.]
    I. Title.
    QL776.J64   1988   88-19175
    591.59—dc19   CIP
                                                                   AC

Manufactured in the United States of America

1 2 3 4 5 6 7 8 9 10 99 98 97 96 95 94 93 92 91 90 89

CONTENTS

INTRODUCTION

Imagine that you are strolling down a woodland path in late afternoon on a warm summer day. As you walk among the trees, you gradually become aware of the animal life all around you. In the branches overhead, you hear a sudden commotion, and moments later, the raucous call of a bluejay fills the air. From the leaf-strewn floor of the woods comes the chirp-chirp-chirp of hidden crickets. In the distance, some squirrels begin chattering noisily in their harsh, rapid-fire fashion.

As shadows lengthen and daylight fades, the first fireflies appear, emitting a pattern of flashes as they weave their way through the vegetation. Finally, as you leave the woods, you spot a rabbit cautiously emerging from the safety of a clump of bushes. The animal carefully sniffs at each tuft of grass or mound of twigs in the vicinity, and then it does

Many kinds of animals, such as this bluejay, communicate by producing sounds.

something rather strange. It rubs its chin back and forth against a large, dead branch lying on the ground. The rabbit waits a moment, then turns quickly to disappear into the underbrush.

7

Fireflies communicate with other members of their species by producing flashes of light. Here, a female firefly (in foreground) is sending a visual signal to male fireflies in the air.

1

COMMUNICATION IN THE ANIMAL WORLD

The various sights and sounds that you have experienced in your walk through the woods are all forms of animal communication. In fact, the woods are filled with messages that are being sent and received by animals of all kinds. Just as we humans need to keep in touch with other people, most animals need to communicate a wide variety of information, particularly to other members of their own species. Such communication is often necessary, for example, in order to determine which animal is the leader of a group. Communication may also be required to locate food, an appropriate place to live, and members of the opposite sex.

Animals communicate in an amazing variety of ways, but generally their communication can be divided into three categories. First, many kinds of animals make sounds to transmit information. The call of a bluejay, the chirp of a cricket, and the chattering of a squirrel are all forms of communication using sound. Not all animal sounds can be detected by human ears. Bats make sounds that are too high for us to hear, while some larger animals such as whales and elephants communicate using some very low sounds that are below the range of human hearing.

A second way in which many animals communicate is by using visual signals. Cats will often signal anger or fear by arching their backs and puffing up their fur. Many kinds of birds use colorful plumage to send visual messages. Male peacocks, for example, spread their long tail feathers into a shimmering fan of color that they use to attract the attention of female peacocks during courtship.

Fireflies have a rather unusual way of sending visual messages. The flashes of light produced by tiny light organs in the insects' bodies are used to locate and attract members of the opposite sex. As a male firefly flies through the night, he produces a characteristic pattern of these light flashes. If a female of the same species sees the signal, she produces a special pattern of flashes in response. The flashing continues as the male gradually moves toward the female, then lands and mates with her.

A third major way in which animals communicate is by producing and releasing chemical substances into the environment. These chemical messages are detected mainly as odors (sometimes as tastes) by other animals. The rather strange behavior of the rabbit that we encountered on our walk in the woods was a form of chemical communication. Rabbits have a gland on their chin that produces an oily secretion. They frequently apply this substance to objects in the area where they live. The odor of the chin-gland secretion lasts for some time and serves as a sign, or marker, to other rabbits. For example, it can communicate the message that a particular area is already inhabited.

At first, it might be hard for us to imagine how a great variety of messages can be transmitted using chemical substances. We humans rely far more on our sight and hearing for communication than on our senses of smell and taste. In fact, in comparison to most other animals, these senses in humans are rather poor. Our noses have between 5 and 10 million tiny receptors for detecting odors. Dogs, on the other hand, are equipped with almost 100 times that many—nearly a billion odor receptors. For dogs and many other animals, the world is filled with an endless array of "odor messages."

Many scientists think that chemical communication—the sending and receiving of chemical messages—may be the primary way by which a great many kinds of animals communicate. In fact, it may be the most widespread form of communication in the animal world.

Chemical communication among animals can take several forms. For example, some animals use foul-smelling chemical secretions for defensive purposes. Their distinctive odors serve as an unmistakable warning to other animals. Skunks are perhaps the most familiar

Predators like the cheetah learn to recognize the odors of animals on which they prey.

animals that communicate this sort of chemical message. The pungent odor of a skunk can be detected from quite a distance. If one whiff of this odor fails to discourage a potential enemy, a skunk can also direct a spray of its smelly secretion at any animal that comes too close. This action usually repels even the most determined attacker.

Odors also play an important role in the relationships between many predators (animals that kill and eat other animals) and their prey (the animals that are killed and eaten). Early in life, many predators learn to recognize the characteristic odors of different kinds of prey animals. When hunting, they follow their noses to their next meal. On the other hand, the odor of a predator usually alarms prey animals and causes them to take evasive action. Some may head for the safety of a burrow or den, while others may try to avoid detection by remaining motionless until the danger has passed.

The first animal pheromone identified by scientists was bombykol, which is produced by female silkworm moths. This chemical helps to bring male and female silkworm moths together for mating.

2

PHEROMONES: THE CHEMICAL SIGNALS OF ANIMALS

By far the most widespread and well-developed form of chemical communication, and the one we shall deal with in this book, is that which takes place between individuals of the same species. This kind of communication involves special chemical signals known as **pheromones**. A pheromone is a chemical, or a mixture of chemicals, that is produced and released by one animal and that brings about a specific response in other animals of the same species. In this way, it acts as a chemical message.

Pheromone research is a relatively new area of science. At the beginning of this century, a number of scientists were investigating the chemical signals that pass between some animals, particularly insects such as moths and butterflies.

Yet it was not until the late 1950s that the first animal pheromone was identified and isolated in the laboratory. In 1959, after many years of work, two German biologists, Erich Hecker and Adolf Butenandt, isolated a pheromone from the silkworm moth. The scientific name for this species of moth is *Bombyx mori*, so Hecker and Butenandt called the pheromone **bombykol**. In their experiments, they had to use more than 500,000 moths to obtain only a few grams of bombykol.

Bombykol acts as a powerful sex attractant. When a female silkworm moth that is ready to mate releases bombykol, she sends a message that spreads rapidly through the air. We humans cannot smell bombykol. But if a male silkworm moth detects the pheromone, his behavior changes almost instantaneously—he stops whatever he is doing and flies off in search of the source of the chemical scent. If the male should lose the trail, he zigzags back and forth through the air until he encounters it again. Eventually he will reach the message-sender and may mate with her. Female silkworm moths that are actively releasing bombykol can attract male moths from as much as one mile (1.6 kilometers) away.

The discovery of bombykol was only the beginning of pheromone research. By the early 1960s, a number of new laboratory techniques were developed that made it possible to probe much deeper into the mysteries of pheromone communication. As a result, there was an almost explosive increase in research. Over the last 25 years, close to 1,000 pheromones have been discovered in a great variety of animals. Quite a few of these compounds have been identified chemically, and some can now be produced in the laboratory. Futhermore, many discoveries have been made concerning how animals actually send and receive these chemical messages.

SENDING PHEROMONE MESSAGES

Pheromones are manufactured in small, specialized structures known as **glands**. Some pheromone glands are relatively simple and are located on or near the surface of an animal's body. Others are more complex; they are found deeper in the body and may have internal reservoirs within which a considerable amount of a pheromone can be stored.

The locations of pheromone glands in animals are remarkably diverse. For instance, the female silkworm moth releases bombykol from a gland located near the tip of her abdomen. The feet of mice and rats are covered with densely packed glands that produce pheromone secretions. Many kinds of deer have small, somewhat circular pheromone glands located immediately in front of and slightly below the inner corners of their eyes. Ants have at least 12 different pheromone-producing glands, ranging from glands in their heads to glands that are associated with their stings.

Pheromones are produced in liquid form. Some pheromone secretions evaporate as soon as they are released and so

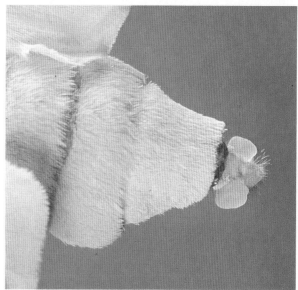

Above: This black-tailed deer is marking a fence post with a pheromone secretion produced by a gland just below its right eye. If you look closely at the photograph, you can see a similar gland below its left eye. *Right:* The pheromone gland of a female silkworm moth is located near the tip of her abdomen.

become quickly dispersed in the air. Others are waxy or oily; such pheromones do not evaporate very fast and so tend to last much longer.

The process of sending a chemical message is a very complex one. Animals normally release pheromones only at certain times, even though they may produce these special chemicals almost continually in their bodies. An animal does not consciously "decide" what pheromone messages to send and when to send them. Rather, it releases pheromones in response to specific **stimuli** (singular, stimulus) that occur either in the world around it or inside its body.

A stimulus is any action or situation that can bring about a reaction in a living thing. For example, an insect might be stimulated to produce a particular pheromone by the presence of an enemy or a potential mate, the act of laying eggs, or the discovery of a rich food source. Only under certain conditions will animals release pheromones and in so doing create a chemical message.

Understanding *why* animals send the kinds of messages that they do is one of the many challenges in pheromone research. Much more is known about *how*

different kinds of animals actually release pheromone molecules into their surroundings. Some animals do so simply by exposing the surface of a gland, perhaps by lifting a tail or wing. Other animals are equipped with accessory structures that help to increase the amount of pheromone they can release or to disperse the pheromone more rapidly.

Some of these structures are quite strange-looking. For example, some types of male butterflies have feathery **scent brushes** (also called **hair pencils**) that they usually keep tucked away inside their bodies in pouches containing pheromone glands. The many fine hairs of scent brushes are saturated with pheromones that attract female butterflies.

When pursuing a female, the male extrudes (pushes out) his scent brushes. Because these delicate structures have a great deal of surface area from which pheromones can evaporate, they act as a sort of chemical radiator, greatly increasing the rate at which pheromone molecules float off into the air. Some species of male moths have long inflatable structures that also help to disperse pheromones.

Above: **The scent brushes of a male queen butterfly extend from the tip of its abdomen.** *Below:* **Some male moths such as the salt marsh moth have inflatable structures called coremata that help to disperse pheromones.**

Another way in which animals communicate using pheromones is to deposit a pheromone secretion on the ground, on some object, or even on another animal. This action creates what is called a **scent mark**. Scent marks have the advantage of communicating information even after the animal making the mark has departed. These pheromone messages serve different purposes. For instance, scent marks can act as a warning to other animals, in effect saying "Keep away!" They also aid in attracting potential mates to an area. When used in this way, they are able to give specific information about the sex, age, and social position of the individual who made the marks.

Some animals leave behind scent marks as they travel from place to place. Many kinds of deer have pheromone glands near the bases of their hooves. With each step, they deposit a scent mark, thus producing a trail of pheromones wherever they go.

Other animals take a more active role in creating scent marks. Rabbits use the pheromone secretion from their chin glands to mark an entire array of objects in their environment. They apply pheromones not only to branches and tufts of

Wolves use urine to create scent marks that communicate information to other wolves.

grass near their home but also to the entrances of their underground burrows, to other adult rabbits in their group, and to their young. They may even stand up on their hind legs to mark high objects. Cats have scent glands around their mouths and on their foreheads. When cats rub their faces against people and objects, they leave behind scent marks that only other cats can detect.

Many animals make scent marks using their own feces or urine. These animals have glands that add pheromones to the waste products as they pass from their bodies. Dogs and wolves are well known for their habit of marking objects with urine. Bison and brown bears urinate on the ground to create pheromone-saturated mud. After rolling in this mud, they rub up against trees, coating trunks and branches with their special pheromone messages.

RECEIVING PHEROMONE MESSAGES

Most animals that have been studied so far detect pheromones with highly sensitive structures called **olfactory receptors**. These receptors are located in different places in different kinds of animals.

In general, vertebrate animals (animals with backbones) have noses with which they investigate odors in the world around them. Inside the nose is an open space, the nasal cavity, that is lined with olfactory receptors. As an animal draws air through its nose, pheromone molecules come into contact with the olfactory receptors and are detected. Fish detect pheromones in their watery world by circulating water through their nasal cavities.

Many kinds of invertebrates (animals without backbones) have a pair of **antennae** projecting from their head. The surface of each antenna is covered with tiny peg-shaped olfactory receptors. The pegs have thin walls that are perforated with small holes called **pores**. Pheromone molecules enter a receptor by way of these pores and are detected inside.

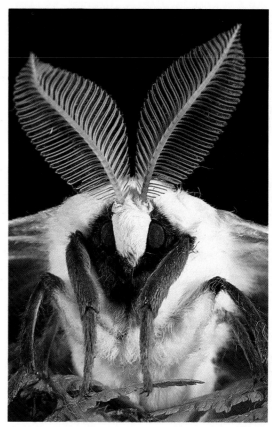

Like many other invertebrates, this luna moth has two antennae that contain pheromone receptors.

The more pores per peg, the more sensitive the olfactory receptor is to various odors in the environment. Grasshoppers, for example, have about 150 pores in each peg, but some male moths have many more. A male silkworm moth has approximately 17,000 pegs on each antenna, with each peg containing up to

19

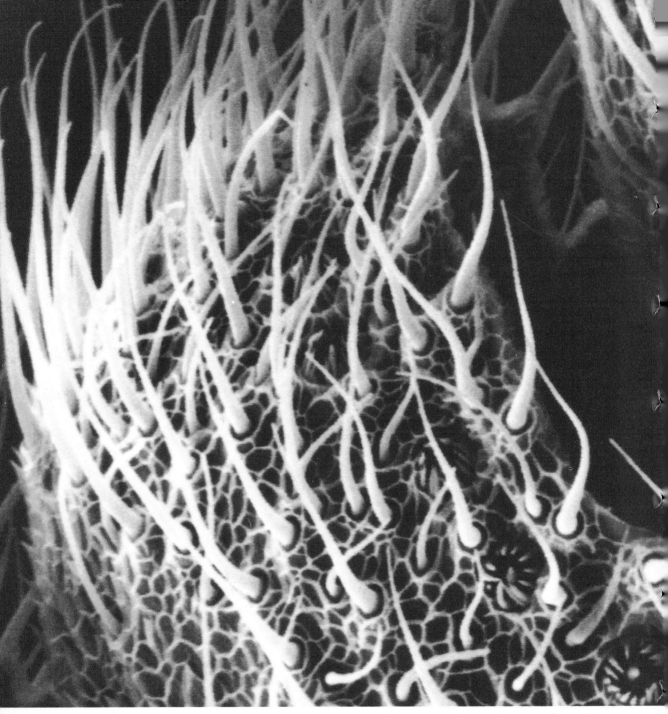

This photograph produced with a scanning electron microscope shows the peg-shaped receptors on the antenna of a male cornborer moth. The image is magnified about 700 times actual size.

3,000 pores. This means that each antenna has close to 50 million pores through which pheromone molecules can pass and be detected!

KINDS OF PHEROMONE MESSAGES

Now that you have an idea of how animals send and receive pheromone messages, let's examine some of the types of messages they are known to exchange.

BRINGING TOGETHER MALES AND FEMALES

A great many kinds of animals release **sex pheromones**. These chemical messages help to bring together male and female animals of the same species so that successful mating can occur. Most sex pheromones, like bombykol, are powerful attractants. Female dogs that are ready to mate give off an odor that has a dramatic effect on male dogs. Males will break their leashes, jump high fences, and travel considerable distances in their efforts to reach a female dog who is broadcasting this pheromone message.

Some animals make sex pheromone "pathways" that potential mates can follow. Certain kinds of female spiders, for instance, spin long lengths of silk that contain pheromones. These delicate silken threads lead male spiders directly to waiting females.

In some species, it is the male rather than the female who releases sex pheromones. In either case, the pheromone signals involved in mating are very complex. Animals respond only to very specific signals sent by members of their particular species.

ATTRACTING A CROWD

Aggregation, or "clustering," **pheromones** cause animals to group together. Aggregation pheromones are particularly widespread in the insect world. Bark beetles, for instance, use a very efficient pheromone communication system when attacking and colonizing a tree.

The first beetle invader to land on a suitable tree releases an aggregation pheromone. This chemical message of invitation spreads quickly, attracting bark beetles of the same species from all directions. In time, thousands of these beetles will alight on the tree and bore through the bark and into the wood. Here they begin constructing the

Attracted to a tree by aggregation pheromones, elm bark beetles construct tunnels in which they live and reproduce.

maze of tunnels in which they will live and reproduce.

PREVENTING OVERCROWDING

Some pheromones stimulate animals to increase the distance between themselves and other members of their species. These are called **dispersal**, or "spacing," **pheromones**.

The female apple maggot fly uses a dispersal pheromone that makes it possible for her offspring to have plenty of food to eat as they develop. Apple maggot flies lay their eggs in fruits such as apples, cherries, and crabapples. After depositing an egg, a female will walk across the surface of the fruit, marking it with dispersal pheromone. If another female apple maggot fly lands on the same fruit, she will respond to this

After laying an egg in an apple, a female apple maggot fly (above) deposits dispersal pheromones that keep other egg-laying females away from the fruit. When the egg hatches, the maggot (below) will have its own food supply.

chemical message by flying away without laying an egg. In this way, the young of each female will have their own supply of fruit and will be assured of having enough food to develop to maturity.

WARNING OF DANGER

Alarm pheromones stimulate a wide range of defensive behaviors, from escaping a source of danger to attacking an unwelcome intruder or predator. Because the chemicals that act as alarm pheromones tend to evaporate into the air very rapidly, the message of alarm can be communicated to other individuals with great speed.

Alarm pheromones released by a threatened or injured animal often cause other animals of the same species to flee. Some kinds of small fish tend to swim together in groups called schools. If one fish is attacked by a predator, it immediately releases an alarm pheromone into the water. This triggers an escape response. The other fish in the school may dart for cover, plummet to the bottom, or swim right at the water's surface in an effort to get away from the source of danger.

Aphids are tiny insects that feed on the sap of green plants. When disturbed or injured, some aphids secrete droplets of a pheromone-containing fluid from projections on their abdomen. As this chemical message of alarm spreads through the air, other aphids nearby will

23

When attacked by a predator such as this nabid bug (left), aphids secrete droplets containing alarm pheromones.

move away or may even drop off the plant in their hurry to escape.

Not all animals beat a hasty retreat when an alarm is raised. Some stand and fight. Bees, ants, and termites often react very aggressively in response to alarm pheromones. Termite soldiers, for example, are the protectors of the termite nest. In some termite species, the soldiers' heads are equipped with "nozzles" for spraying alarm pheromones on invaders. The pheromone secretion excites and alerts other soldiers and prepares them to attack. As an added benefit, the secretion is sticky and irritating, and it helps to immobilize the intruders.

DUELING WITH PHEROMONES

Often a tense situation can arise when two animals of the same species that are strangers to each other come together. Their encounter may lead to aggressive behavior that involves signaling and threatening with odors.

Such encounters often take place among lemurs, agile animals related to monkeys. Lemurs live only on the island of Madagascar, off the southeastern coast of Africa. When two male lemurs that are strangers cross paths, they sometimes engage in a rather bizarre activity called a "stink fight."

To prepare for a stink fight, lemurs

The ring-tailed lemurs of Madagascar use pheromone secretions in a strange kind of competition called a stink fight.

spread pheromone secretions over themselves and their immediate surroundings. They coat their hands, feet, and even their tails with pheromone secretions produced by special glands on their chests and wrists. Now armed with odors, the two animals approach each other, waving their freshly scented tails in the air and making scent marks on the surrounding vegetation with their pheromone-covered hands and feet. One animal may advance a little and then retreat as the other comes toward him. Each time a lemur advances, he takes care to place his own pheromone marks directly over those of the other lemur, thus destroying the scent of his opponent in that spot. The fight may go back and forth like this for more than an hour before one animal eventually gives up and retreats for good.

MAKING A TRAIL

Pheromones can be released into the air or deposited on a surface to form a trail that other animals can follow. A wide variety of animals, including ants, snails, and snakes, lay pheromone trails.

Trail pheromones in ants have been studied extensively. As an ant scurries along, it can deposit pheromone secretions from a variety of glands on its legs and abdomen. These trails are used to show the way to food sources, to direct other ants to a new location for a nest, or to help the trail-laying individual find its way back home. Unlike alarm pheromones, which tend to disperse rapidly, trail pheromones are much more persistent and the chemical messages they convey last much longer.

RECOGNIZING PLACES AND PARENTS

Being able to recognize one's home, parents, or members of one's group is necessary for the survival of many animals, and pheromones play an important role in this recognition. For instance, bees appear to recognize their own nest by its characteristic smell. Many substances probably contribute to this "colony odor," but the types and amounts of pheromones present certainly are important components.

Recognition pheromones also seem to be necessary in establishing and maintaining bonds between members of a group of animals, especially between females and their young. Members of a herd of black-tailed deer recognize one

Members of a herd of black-tailed deer recognize one another by the distinctive odor of each deer's tarsal gland pheromones.

another by the odor of pheromones secreted from their tarsal glands (located on the insides of the knees of the rear legs.) The tarsal gland secretions of each individual are slightly different from those of other members of the group and so serve as a form of identification. Fawns use these pheromones to identify their mothers among the female deer in the herd. A fawn may sniff the tarsal glands of a number of females before finding the correct one.

A COMPLEX SYSTEM OF COMMUNICATION

Although pheromones are known to exist in hundreds of animal species, scientists are still just beginning to understand how this system of chemical communication works. With each new discovery, it becomes more and more obvious that pheromone communication is far more complex than early investigators ever imagined. For a time after the discovery of bombykol, many researchers thought that each pheromone was a single chemical compound that communicated one kind of chemical message. But as scientists have continued to look into the chemical language of animals, they have found that, in many species, some pheromones are made up of not just one or two, but many chemical compounds that are precisely blended and balanced. Each component contributes to the overall meaning of the message. Some beaver pheromones, for example, may contain as many as 50 different substances. The proportions of these chemicals in the pheromone mixture vary somewhat from beaver to beaver, almost like a chemical signature.

Futhermore, researchers now know that pheromone communication is more complex in some kinds of animals than in others. In the insect world, for example, pheromones generally trigger very predictable, almost automatic responses. In fact, many insects have been compared to tiny machines: when exposed to a particular pheromone, they will respond to it in the same way time after time. But this is not the case with other animals, especially mammals. Their responses to pheromones are more complex. In fact, it seems that, among mammals, the same pheromone can mean different things under different circumstances.

To complicate matters even more, environmental factors such as temperature, humidity, light intensity, and the time of day or year also affect how pheromone messages are sent and interpreted in a wide variety of animal species.

In order to really understand the role that pheromone communication plays in an animal's life, it is important to know as much as possible about how that animal behaves. Studying large animals in the wild is often difficult. For one thing, animals such as wolves or deer move from place to place, sometimes covering great distances in a short period of time. For this and other reasons, many scientists involved in pheromone research have focused their studies on animals

Using hives with glass walls, scientists can observe the way in which honey bees communicate with each other.

whose behavior can be observed more easily, often right in the laboratory.

One of the best-studied systems of pheromone communication in animals is that of the honey bee. Honey bees that live in temperate climates (areas with cold winters and warm summers) are almost ideal subjects for pheromone research. These bees build their nests inside enclosed places, such as holes in trees, spaces in walls, or boxlike hives provided by beekeepers. By constructing hives with glass walls, scientists have been able to watch bees inside their nests and observe firsthand how they interact and communicate with one another.

Now that you have a little background on pheromones, let's take a look at how important pheromone communication is for the members of a honey bee colony and how these chemical messages play a role in almost every aspect of a bee's life.

A queen honey bee surrounded by worker bees

3

THE WORLD OF THE
HONEY BEE

A single honey bee, living alone, would quickly die. Honey bees must live together in order to survive. Like ants, termites, and many kinds of wasps, honey bees are social insects. In fact, honey bees have one of the most complex social organizations in the insect world. They live together in large groups known as colonies. A honey bee colony can exist for years, growing and then dividing over and over again.

Usually between 20,000 and 60,000 bees live in an average-size honey bee colony. With that many bees living together in a relatively small, enclosed space, you might think that life in the nest would be disorderly, even confused. But this is not the case at all. The bees cooperate with each other in a very organized way as they carry out a wide

variety of tasks. Pheromones play a very important role in that cooperation.

At first glance, all the bees in a colony might look pretty much the same, but there are actually three distinct types of bees. Each type—queen, worker, and drone—has a specific role to play in the busy community in which it lives.

In each honey bee colony, there is a single **queen bee**. The queen is larger than the other bees, with a longer, narrower abdomen. She spends almost all of her time laying eggs. In fact, she is normally the only bee in the colony that does lay eggs. The queen is remarkably efficient at her job. During the spring and early summer, she may lay as many as 3,000 eggs per day! And since a queen can live for several years, during her lifetime she will lay hundreds of thousands of eggs.

QUEEN **WORKER** **DRONE**

A honey bee colony contains three types of bees. The queen bee (left) has a long, narrow abdomen that is rather pointed at the end. Worker bees (center) are the smallest type of bee in the colony. Drones (right) have thick, stocky bodies, powerful wings, and enormous eyes.

Most of the other bees in the nest are **workers**. Workers are the smallest of the three types of bees in the colony. All worker bees are female, but unlike the queen, they do not normally lay eggs. Instead, the workers perform the multitude of other tasks necessary for the colony to exist.

The particular job that a worker performs seems to depend to a large extent on her age. For example, one of a young worker's first jobs is to keep the nest clean. As she matures somewhat, she becomes a nurse bee that tends eggs and feeds developing bees. Worker bees also feed the queen. Because the queen does not find food for herself, she is dependent on other members of the colony to take care of her needs. When workers are near their queen, they respond to her presence by feeding her and grooming her body. They also look after the many eggs she lays.

When a worker is slightly more than a week old, she begins to secrete tiny pieces of wax from wax glands on the underside of her abdomen. Using these wafer-like bits of wax, workers construct the combs that form the architectural framework of their nest.

A typical honey bee nest has several combs that hang vertically inside the nest cavity. Each comb is made up of thousands of small, hexagonal (six-sided) wax chambers called **cells**. In each comb, the cells are arranged into two layers that lie back to back, with the open ends of the cells facing out. The hexagonal cells of the comb are the tiny chambers into which the queen lays eggs that will develop into new workers or male bees. These cells are also used by the honey bees as storage containers for their food.

At certain times, worker bees may also build **queen cells**, a very different kind of cell in which young queen bees are raised. Queen cells are much larger than the other cells of the comb. They have an irregular, acornlike shape and project from the combs' surface.

Queen cells are irregularly shaped and project from the surface of the comb.

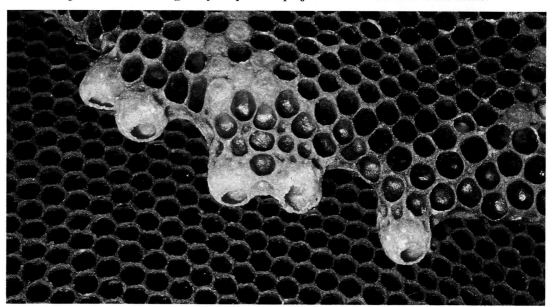

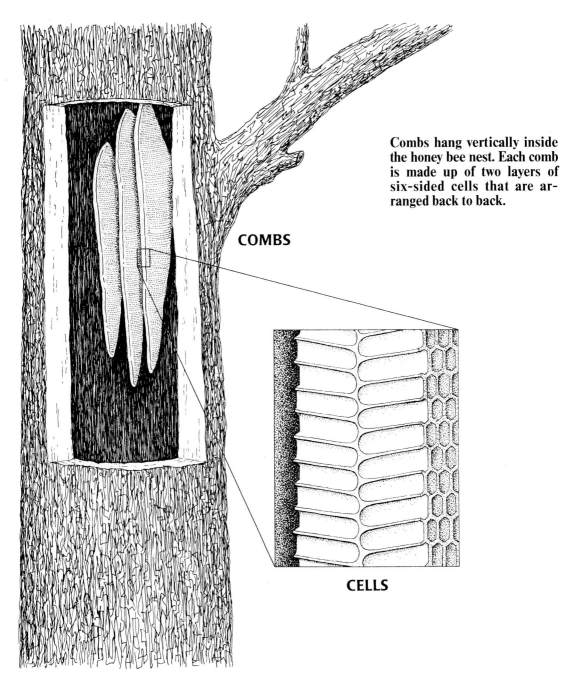

Combs hang vertically inside the honey bee nest. Each comb is made up of two layers of six-sided cells that are arranged back to back.

COMBS

CELLS

34

A foraging bee searches for nectar in a thistle flower. Notice the yellow pollen stored in special pouches on her legs.

When worker bees are about three weeks old, they take on a new job. They become foragers. Foragers are the food-gatherers of the colony; they regularly fly out from the nest in search of flowers. From flowers, honey bees take two things—nectar and pollen. The nectar that they bring back to the nest will be converted by other workers into honey. This sweet, golden liquid is then stored in row upon row of cells on the comb. Pollen is a protein-rich food for bees. Whatever is not used immediately is packed and stored in other cells for future use.

The average worker bee lives about six weeks, a very brief life by human standards. During that time, she will have performed many different jobs. In contrast, male bees, or **drones**, have little to do with the day-to-day life and work of the

A male honey bee, or drone (center), can be recognized by his large eyes and thick body.

colony. Drones are the third type of bee in the honey bee community. They have rather thick, compact bodies, and enormous eyes. A typical honey bee colony usually contains several hundred drones.

Drones spend most of their time simply standing around inside the nest or begging for food from passing worker bees. But during one period of their lives,

drones have a very important role to play: they mate with young queen bees when they leave the nest on their mating flights. A queen that has never mated is able to lay eggs, but those eggs will always develop into drones. Only after a queen has mated with a drone can she lay eggs that will develop into workers and new queens. Drones die within minutes of mating, but they will have fulfilled their vital function in the life of the honey bee colony.

Whether it is a drone, a worker, or a queen, each and every honey bee begins its life as a tiny, fragile egg in the bottom of a cell on the comb. Three days after the egg is laid, a white, wormlike **larva** hatches out of it. For the next week, nurse bees feed the larva almost continually, and it grows very rapidly. After only 24 hours, the larva weighs five and a half times as much as it did when it hatched!

For the first three days after hatching, all larvae are fed a rich, milky white substance called royal jelly. Royal jelly is secreted from special food-producing glands in the heads of worker bees. On the third day, the food of larvae that will develop into drones and workers is changed. Instead of royal jelly, they are

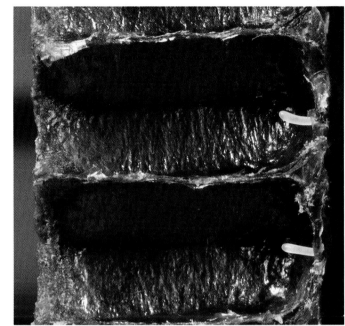

Right: This cross-section photograph shows tiny white eggs on the bottom of cells in a honey bee comb. *Below:* The larvae that hatch from the eggs grow quickly and soon become so large that they almost fill their cells.

fed a mixture of honey and pollen. Larvae destined to become queens, however, continue to receive a steady diet of royal jelly.

By the sixth day, most of the larvae have grown so large that they practically fill their wax chambers. At this point, workers seal each larva in its cell, along with a little extra food. They seal the cells by closing each one with a slightly rounded cap of wax. Once shut inside its cell, the larva spins a silky cocoon. Then it begins to change from a worm-like larva into a **pupa**.

A pupa does not eat, but remains very still inside the cell. As time passes, the pupa's body undergoes many changes and gradually comes to look more and more like the body of an adult bee. At first, the pupa is white and delicate, with its newly formed wings and legs folded tightly against its body. But as the transformation from pupa to young bee progresses, the white body becomes more darkly colored. When the changes in its body are finally completed, the young bee, now fully developed, chews its way through the wax cap of its cell and crawls out onto the comb. It stretches its folded wings, ready to begin life as an adult.

Within their wax-capped cells, pupae gradually develop into young honey bees. In this photograph, the caps have been removed from the cells so that you can see the pupae inside.

38

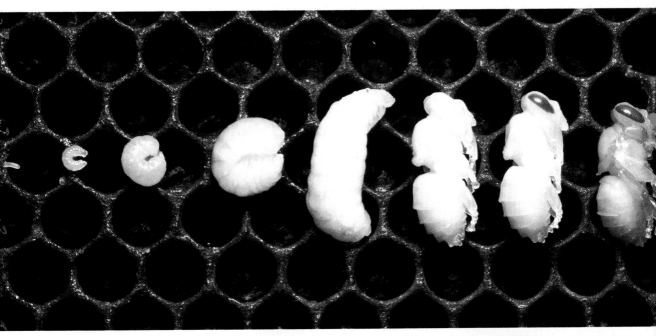

After going through a process of development from egg to larva to pupa (above), a young bee emerges from its cell and crawls out onto the comb (right).

39

COMMUNICATION IN THE HONEY BEE COLONY

As each new honey bee emerges from its cell, it automatically takes its place alongside thousands of nestmates in the amazingly organized life of the colony. What is also amazing is that, inside the nest, all of this coordinated activity takes place in the dark!

After years of careful study, it is now apparent that the secret to the bees' organization is an extensive and complex system of communication. At any given moment, bees in a colony are sending and receiving many messages. They are constantly exchanging information with the other members of their society and gathering information from their immediate surroundings.

Inside their dark nest, bees depend very little on their sight. They do rely on their sense of touch, however. Honey bees frequently touch one another with their antennae, legs, and mouth parts. During this physical contact, they can exchange information directly. Bees also make a variety of sounds that other bees near them can hear and respond to.

Bee "dancing" is a rather well-known form of honey bee communication that involves both touching and sound production. Bees perform elaborate movements called **dances** on the surface of the comb. In these dances, they walk, circle, make buzzing sounds, fan their wings, and vibrate their bodies in certain ways. Workers crowd around a dancing bee and feel its movements with their antennae. Each part of the dance has meaning and conveys information to the surrounding bees.

But even more impressive than bee "dancing" is the honey bees' extremely elaborate system of pheromone communication. It may be that almost all of a bee's activities are carried out in response to pheromone messages.

Pheromones are an ideal form of communication for honey bees. If bees could communicate only by touching each other or by making tiny sounds, just a few bees at a time would be involved. These bees, in turn, would have to stop whatever they were doing and pass the information on to other bees in the same way. In a colony containing tens of thousands of bees, information would travel very slowly by these methods alone. But by releasing chemical mes-

Foraging bees communicate information about food sources by performing special dances on the comb surface. This dancing bee is carrying loads of pollen on both hind legs.

sages into the air, bees can communicate with all the members of the colony in an extremely short time. And it is this kind of rapid communication that helps to keep all the activities in the nest running so smoothly.

Communicating with chemical mes-sages works especially well inside the bees' nest. Because the nest is enclosed, the wind cannot blow the pheromones away. By rapidly fanning their wings, the bees can control how fast their chemical messages are spread. Old messages are cleared away by wingfanning as well.

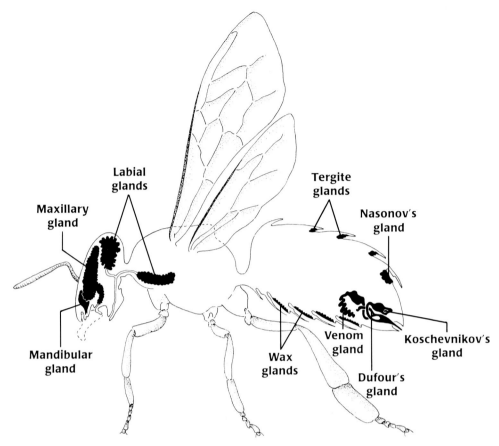

Honey bees have a variety of glands, several of which are shown here. Most of these glands are associated with pheromone production.

THE PHEROMONES OF HONEY BEES

All honey bees produce certain kinds of pheromones. Scientists have identified nearly a dozen different glands that are involved in producing these important chemicals. Most pheromone glands are located on the bee's head, thorax (the middle portion of the body), and abdo-men. There are also glands on the legs and feet.

Using pheromones, bees are able to communicate a truly remarkable amount of information. Many researchers have spent years trying to understand this chemical "language" of honey bees. Although much remains a mystery, some of the bees' chemical messages have been identified and decoded.

A honey bee exposing her Nasonov scent gland. At the same time, she fans her wings to help spread the chemical message.

NASONOV PHEROMONE

Honey bees have a gland near the tip of their abdomen called the **Nasonov scent gland** (named after the Russian scientist who first described it in 1883). The pheromone produced by this gland is very attractive to bees. It has a rather pleasant, somewhat sweet odor (to the human nose at least). When honey bees detect this pheromone, they are strongly attracted to it.

By releasing Nasonov pheromone, a bee can attract other bees to a specific location. For example, if the weather is

hot and a worker bee finds a source of clean water, she will communicate this information to other members of her colony by flexing the tip of her abdomen slightly downward and exposing her Nasonov gland to the air. Then as the pheromone is released from the gland, she rapidly fans her wings. As other bees detect the pheromone, they fly off toward its source. When they locate the bee that is sending the message, they land near her and quickly find the water.

ALARM PHEROMONES

The tasty and nutritious stores of honey and pollen inside a honey bee nest are quite tempting to other animals, including bees from other colonies. To protect the colony and its food reserves, alert guard bees constantly patrol the nest entrance. When a guard is disturbed in some way, she releases an alarm pheromone by slightly protruding her sting. While fanning her wings, she runs into the nest. Other bees quickly detect the alarm pheromone and become excited and aggressive. They hurry to the nest entrance with their wings extended and antennae waving, ready to attack.

When a bee actually stings an animal,

43

Guard bees attacking a wasp that has invaded their nest. Alarm pheromones stimulate bees to attack and sting an intruder.

the alarm pheromones that are released in the process also serve to mark the object being stung as the target of the attack. Other bees respond to this powerful chemical message by angrily stinging whatever the first bee stung.

Intruders in the nest are usually overpowered or driven off by such an attack. Once the alarm pheromone has been released, the message travels quickly through the colony. Within seconds, enough bees will usually arrive on the scene to prevent damage to the nest or its inhabitants.

OTHER HONEY BEE PHEROMONES

There may be other kinds of pheromones at work inside a honey bee colony. Larvae and pupae developing inside the cells of the comb probably give off pheromones that stimulate nurse bees to feed and care for them. Since larvae of different ages are fed different amounts of food, it may be that a change in a larva's pheromone secretions causes nurse bees to change the larva's diet.

Honey bee workers also deposit trail pheromones. Bees entering the nest, for example, mark the entrance with a trail pheromone. This probably helps them and their fellow foragers to find the entrance each time they return from a food-gathering trip. Bees also use trail pheromones to mark particularly rich sources of food.

Some scientists speculate that many other honey bee activities also involve pheromone messages. For instance, bees performing dances on the comb may release pheromone messages that supplement the information communicated by the dancer's movements. Dying bees may even release a chemical signal that stimulates special "undertaker" bees to remove dead individuals from the nest.

MESSAGES FROM THE QUEEN

For many years, beekeepers, as well as scientists who studied bees, noticed that there is something very special about the queen bee. If a single worker or a drone is removed from the nest, nothing happens. The other bees seem not to notice. But if the queen is removed from her colony, order in the nest breaks down. In a very short time, the smoothly running honey bee society becomes a mass of confused, excited bees.

The queen is the most important bee in the honey bee colony. Without her, the colony could not exist. She influences all the other bees and almost everything that happens in the nest. How is the queen able to do this?

The queen produces a special set of pheromones that none of the other bees makes. Using these special pheromones, she is able to send many different kinds of messages to the members of her colony. When workers and drones receive these messages from the queen, they respond to them in very characteristic ways. For example, queen pheromones seem to stimulate workers to build

45

combs, look after developing bees in the nest, forage for nectar and pollen, and store food. In a sense, it is almost as if the queen "controls" the other bees in the colony by the chemical messages she sends.

In order for the all-important pheromone messages of the queen to reach the many thousands of bees in the colony, they must be well distributed throughout the nest. Some queen pheromones probably evaporate fairly quickly from her body and become dispersed in the atmosphere of the hive. Others are more long-lasting and seem to be spread through the colony by workers in a most interesting way.

As the queen stands on the surface of the comb, she is almost always surrounded by a circle of 8 to 12 worker bees. This group of workers is called the queen's "court." Each time a worker leaves the court, another bee will step in to take her place. In addition to offering the queen food and licking her body, members of the queen's court constantly touch the queen with their antennae. It seems that during this process, queen pheromones are transferred to the antennae of the encircling workers, who in turn transfer them to other colony members. The result is that the pheromone messages of the queen are kept constantly circulating among the tens of thousands of individuals in the honey bee nest.

The best-studied of the queen's pheromones are those secreted from her mandibular glands, located near her mouth. A major chemical component of mandibular-gland secretion was isolated and identified in 1960. This chemical, called **queen substance**, can be produced in the laboratory and is often used in experiments on bee behavior.

The mandibular gland pheromones of the queen are involved in a wide variety of bee behaviors. For instance, they seem to be the pheromones that stimulate members of the queen's court to feed and groom her. These pheromones also enable workers to recognize that a particular bee is indeed a queen. Scientists have found that if they paint queen mandibular gland pheromones on an ordinary worker bee, other bees in the vicinity will suddenly treat her as if she were a queen. Within approximately 10 minutes, however, this new "chemical identity" will fade, and the worker will

A queen bee surrounded by the members of her court. Notice how some of the worker bees are touching the queen's body with their antennae.

once again be treated like an ordinary bee by her nestmates.

The queen's pheromones affect not only the behavior of workers but also their bodies. Remember that although workers are female, they normally do not lay eggs. This is because queen pheromones (possibly queen substance in particular) prevent their reproductive organs from developing. In this way, the queen can maintain her position as the only egg-laying female in the nest.

Drones, like workers, seem to recognize a queen by her special pheromones. A young, unmated queen releases a trail of pheromones (including queen substance) as she flies out of the nest on her mating flight. Drones are strongly attracted by this chemical message in the air, and they quickly fly off in pursuit of the queen. In experiments, scientists have put a small amount of queen pheromones on wooden models of queen bees. Then they suspended the models from balloons and "flew" them through the air. Drones followed the pheromone-coated models just as if they were real queens. Sometimes drones even tried to mate with the models!

The chemical messages sent by the queen bee are clearly very important in keeping the day-to-day life of the nest running smoothly. But the queen's pheromones also play a key role in one of the most spectacular events that occurs in the life of a honey bee colony. That event is swarming.

PHEROMONES AND SWARMING

During the winter months, a queen bee does not lay eggs. She and other members of the colony spend their time and energy just keeping warm inside the nest. With the arrival of spring, however, the queen starts laying eggs once again, and soon the size of the colony begins to increase. With the queen laying eggs at the rate of several thousand per day, it doesn't take long for the number of bees in the nest to become very large. And you can imagine how, in the limited space of the nest cavity, the bees become more and more crowded. When the crowding becomes extreme, it is time for the colony to divide.

Honey bee colonies divide by a process known as **swarming.** A swarm is an enormous group of thousands of bees that leave the nest together to start a new colony in a new location. For many years, people have puzzled over the swarming process. What stimulates the bees to divide their colony? How is swarming coordinated so that thousands of individual bees stay together once they are outside the nest? How do they all "know" what to do and where to go?

As a result of much research, scientists are beginning to understand some of the details in this rather mysterious process. Not surprisingly, the queen bee and her pheromone messages play a central role in it.

In an uncrowded bee nest, there is

plenty of space. All the bees, including the queen, are free to walk all around the nest. Every day the queen walks over the combs, laying eggs. As she walks, she leaves behind more than just her eggs. With every step, she also deposits an oily, colorless trail of pheromones on the surface of the comb. These chemical "footprints" contain yet another message for the worker bees. The queen's footprint pheromone, when combined with other queen pheromones, somehow keeps the workers from building queen cells, the large, acorn-shaped chambers in which new queen bees are raised.

As the population of the colony increases and the nest becomes more and more crowded, however, the situation changes. Bees are now tightly packed on the combs, especially near the edges. The queen cannot walk freely all around the nest as she did before. And where she cannot walk, she cannot leave her "footprints." Futhermore, such crowded conditions may prevent other queen pheromones from being distributed throughout the nest as they normally are. The result of this change of signals is that workers begin to build queen cells along the edges of the combs.

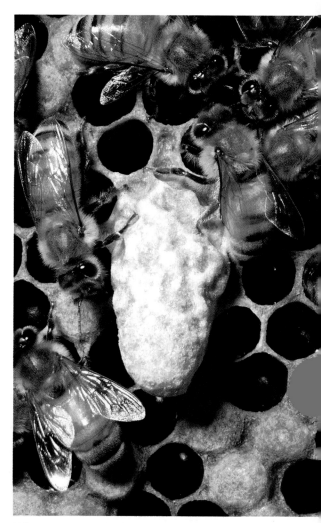

When a honey bee colony becomes too crowded, workers build cells in which new queens will develop.

When several queen cells are constructed, the workers make room for the queen to approach the cells. In fact, some of the workers may actually push her toward these large cells, if she seems reluctant to go. The queen then lays an egg in each one.

The larvae that hatch from these eggs are destined to become new queens. They are fed large quantities of royal jelly by the workers. As a result of this rich diet, they grow quickly. Then, when the time is right, workers seal each larva inside its bulging wax chamber.

The fact that new queens are developing in the nest is a signal to all members of the colony that the time for swarming is very near. It may be that the developing queens secrete pheromones through their wax cells. These chemical messages might then be detected by nurse bees and spread throughout the colony.

Two or three days before the new queens are ready to emerge from their cells, a group of scout bees leaves the nest. Scout bees are experienced foragers, but now they are not searching for nectar or pollen. They fly off in all directions to look for a proper location for a new home. Scouts spend considerable time

Sealed with a wax cap, each of these queen cells contains a developing queen bee.

investigating dark holes and large cracks in trees and walls. They will explore old buildings and even empty boxes as they search for a site that is just right for a bees' nest.

Each time scouts return to the nest, they inform the other bees about their discoveries by performing special dances on the surface of the comb. The dances contain information about the location of new nesting sites. Scouts may also communicate additional information by releasing pheromones while dancing.

Deep inside the nest, another kind of communicating is going on. While the maturing queens are still sealed inside their cells, the old queen sometimes produces a "tooting" sound by vibrating her body in a particular way. The new queens respond from inside their cells by making a "quacking" sound.

This communication between the old queen and the new queens is important. If a new queen comes out of her cell before the old queen leaves with the swarm, the two queens will fight each other. Only one will survive this battle. By "tooting" and "quacking," the queens keep track of each other and avoid this deadly combat.

Shortly before the new queens are ready to emerge from their cells, a strange calm descends on the colony. Scouts stop dancing; foraging bees stop looking for food; and workers inside the nest stop performing their many chores.

Suddenly, it seems that a signal passes among the scouts. Perhaps this signal has to do with pheromones, but no one really knows. Now, instead of dances, the scouts make short runs on the comb. As they run, they produce a peculiar buzzing sound with their wings. These buzzing runs excite nearby bees who also begin to run and buzz like the scouts. The excitement passes through the colony like a chain reaction. Soon all the bees in the nest are buzzing and moving rapidly about on the combs. Then, all at once, the bees stream out of the nest entrance in a great rush, taking the old queen with them. Only the very youngest bees stay behind.

For a few moments, thousands of bees fill the air. Then some of the airborne bees, together with the queen, head away from the nest. As the queen flies, she releases queen substance and possibly other queen pheromones as well. The bees with her release Nasonov pheromone

This swarm of honey bees has left the nest, taking their queen with them.

from their scent glands. Leaving a trail of pheromones behind it, the swarm settles nearby, usually on a tree branch or some other firm object.

The first bees to settle vigorously fan their wings as they continue to release Nasonov pheromone. Many bees still flying around in the air are attracted by this pheromone message, and they alight on the branch to join the now-clustered swarm. Yet for some reason (no one really understands why), not all of the airborne bees continue with the swarm. Some return to the nest, where they land near the entrance. Still other bees remain in the air, flying back and forth.

Then a strange sort of competition takes place. Bees in the clustered swarm with the queen continue to release Nasonov pheromone from their scent glands. At the same time, the bees that returned to the nest also release Nasonov pheromone. It is almost as if the two groups of bees are competing for the remaining bees still flying around in the air.

Eventually, about half the bees that left the nest stay with the swarm. The rest return to the nest, where they will wait for one of the young queens to emerge. Since the colony usually has only one queen, the first new queen to crawl out of her cell onto the comb has an advantage. She quickly locates the remaining queen cells and kills the other young queens by stinging them to death. If two queens emerge at the same time, they will fight until one is dead. The surviving queen then takes her place as the queen of the colony. In a few days she will fly out of the nest, mate, and then return to begin her lifelong career of laying eggs.

Meanwhile, there is a great deal of activity going on in the clustered swarm. Although from the outside this great clump of bees looks like mass confusion, it is actually quite organized. On the inside, the bees cling to one another to form living chains. There is enough space between the chains so other bees can move about. A solid mass of bees forms a covering about three bees thick around this loosely spaced interior. There is an opening in this covering of bees through which individuals can fly into and out of the cluster.

From the swarm, scout bees fly out to resume their search for a new nest site. Each time a scout bee returns, she performs a dance on the outside of the clustered swarm. The dance contains specific information about a site that the bee has visited, such as its distance from the swarm and the direction the bees must fly to reach it. Scientists have found that scouts returning from the most suitable locations for a new nest dance most vigorously and for the longest period of time. Sometimes scouts will also mark a particularly good site with Nasonov pheromone. This attracts other scouts. After closely inspecting the site, they too may dance in favor of that site when they return to the swarm.

A clustered swarm of bees on a tree branch

If you could watch the scouts dancing, you would notice that as time passes, more and more scouts dance the same dance. No one understands exactly how it happens, but somehow the scouts eventually "agree" on a location for the new nest site. How the bees reach this "decision" is still one of the great mysteries of honey bee life. It is quite likely that the process involves complex chemical messages that pass among the scouts and possibly the rest of the bees as well.

Once the choice is made, scouts perform buzzing runs on the surface of the clustered swarm. This stimulates all the bees to fly up into the air together. Once airborne, they head toward their new home.

As the swarm flies, the scouts seem to lead the way, possibly by releasing Nasonov pheromone. Yet, as before, the queen's presence coordinates the bees' actions. All the bees in the swarm know that their queen is with them because they continually detect her pheromones in the air. Without the queen and her pheromone messages to coordinate it, the swarm cannot continue its flight.

Scientists have demonstrated this by imprisoning the queen in a small wire cage so she cannot fly with the swarm. When the scouts give the signal, the bees lift off, but they fly only a short distance. As soon as they sense that their queen is not with them, they return to her. They will lift off again and again, but as long as the queen stays behind, the swarm will not complete the journey to its new nest site.

Similarly, if a swarm accidentally loses its queen during the flight, the bees quickly become restless and disorganized. For many hours, they will search for their queen. If they cannot find her, most of the bees will fly back to the original nest. Those that do not will soon die.

Most of the time, however, a swarm does reach its new nest site without mishap. When the bees arrive at their destination, they release Nasonov pheromone and fan their wings. Perhaps this helps to attract any stragglers. Work begins immediately, and within a few days, new combs have been constructed, foragers are flying out in search of food, and the queen has begun to lay eggs once again. In less than a week after they swarmed, the bees are settled in their new home.

Researchers are looking for ways in which pheromones can be used to control insect pests like this corn earworm.

4

WHY STUDY PHEROMONES?

Pheromone communication is a fascinating part of honey bee life. In many ways, however, we are only beginning to understand it—much remains to be discovered and explained.

One of the most exciting (and sometimes frustrating!) things about any area of science is that the more we know, the more it seems there is to know. Yet as scientists continue to investigate pheromone communication, they are doing more than satisfying their curiosity. There are very practical reasons for studying the pheromones of honey bees, as well as those of other animals. The knowledge we gain from such research can be used to benefit humans in a variety of ways.

ATTRACTING HELPFUL INSECTS

As they forage for food, bees and other insects spread pollen from flower to flower. In so doing, they insure that many kinds of plants will continue to produce seeds year after year, seeds that will grow into the plants that provide us with food and other useful products. It might some day be possible to use synthetic pheromones to make these insect pollinators more efficient. In the future, for instance, farmers may be able to attract bees to crops that need pollinating by spraying their fields with synthetic Nasonov pheromone.

Researchers at the U. S. Department of Agriculture conducting an experiment with the trail pheromones of fire ants. The pheromones might be used to attract the insects to food treated with insecticide, which would then be carried back to the nest and consumed. This is only one of the ways in which pheromones may be helpful in controlling insect pests.

FIGHTING INSECT PESTS

Not all insects are as helpful as honey bees. Almost one-third of all human food grown each year is destroyed by insect pests. For decades, the only way to control such insects has been to use toxic chemicals (insecticides) to kill them. But insecticides have been far from a perfect solution. Over the years, many kinds of insects have developed a resistance to these chemicals so that they are no longer effective. Futhermore, countless numbers of beneficial insects such as bees and wasps are needlessly destroyed by the use of insecticides, and the health of other animals in the environment (including humans) is endangered. For these reasons, many researchers are currently trying to discover ways in which pheromones can be used to control insect pests.

One strategy has been to try to reduce communication between male and female insects of a particular species in the hope of interfering with the normal mating process. This is done by spraying an area with female sex attractant pheromones. The idea is to "confuse" the male insects so they have difficulty finding the opposite sex. Unfortunately, this approach has not

Attracted by an aggregation phero-mone, grain weevils have been caught in an oily substance con-tained in the center of this trap. Such pheromone-baited traps may be useful in monitoring in-sect populations.

been very successful, probably because mating is an extremely complex process controlled by many factors.

Other researchers have tried to catch large numbers of insect pests in traps baited with pheromones. The results of this strategy have also been disappoint-ing. In 1979, for example, scientists in Norway and Sweden set up over 600,000 pheromone-baited traps in forests where spruce beetles were damaging the trees. In a two-year period, nearly 8 billion spruce beetles were caught in these traps, and yet the trees continued to be de-stroyed at almost the same rate as they were before the trapping took place.

Probably the most successful approach in the war against insect pests has been to use pheromone-baited traps as a kind of early warning system to monitor insect populations in a particular area. If the population grows too large, insecticides can then be applied at just the right time to kill the maximum number of harmful insects and yet do the least amount of damage to other animals in the environ-ment. This technique seems to work quite well and is now used to control a wide variety of insect pests such as boll weevils that attack fields of cotton and gypsy moths that damage and even de-stroy entire forests.

UNDERSTANDING ANIMALS —AND OURSELVES?

What we learn from pheromone research enables us to do more than simply alter the behavior of some animals. It opens up a whole new way of looking at the world around us. For a long time, our understanding of animal behavior was based on what we could see or hear animals doing. The study of chemical communication has greatly expanded our knowledge of how many kinds of animals interact with one another. It has also helped to solve many of the mysteries surrounding behavior in a variety of animal species. Each new discovery is much like fitting one more piece into an enormous jigsaw puzzle. It now seems that we can hardly claim to understand an animal's actions without knowing something about the chemical messages that the animal is sending and receiving.

Finally, there is a possibility that there may be human pheromones, too. A number of researchers are investigating this intriguing, and very controversial, idea. Perhaps someday we may discover that, like honey bees, rabbits, dogs, and so many other kinds of animals, we humans have our own special chemical messages that may communicate as much information as a spoken word or a cheerful smile.

GLOSSARY

aggregation pheromones—chemical messages that cause animals of the same species to come together in groups

alarm pheromones—chemical messages that stimulate animals to defend themselves and their group or to flee from danger

antennae (an-TEN-ee)—sense organs on the heads of insects and other invertebrates where receptors that detect pheromones are located. The singular form of the word is **antenna (an-TEN-uh).**

bombykol (BOHM-bih-kol)—a sex pheromone produced by the silkworm moth, *Bombyx mori*

cells—the six-sided wax chambers in a bee nest where young worker and male bees develop and where food is stored

dances—special patterns of movement and sound used by honey bees to communicate information to other bees

dispersal pheromones—chemical messages that cause animals to increase the distance between themselves and other members of the same species

drones (DROHNS)—male bees in a honey bee colony

glands—specialized structures in the bodies of animals that produce pheromones and other chemical substances

hair pencils—specialized organs used by some kinds of male butterflies to disperse pheromones. Hair pencils (also known as **scent brushes**) are covered with fine hairs that make it possible for the chemicals to evaporate rapidly.

larva—the worm-like second stage in the development of bees and many other insects. Bee larvae **(LAHR-vee)** are small and white.

Nasonov scent gland—a gland in honey bees that produces Nasonov pheromone, which is very attractive to bees. The gland and the pheromone are named after a 19th-century Russian scientist.

olfactory (ol-FAK-tuh-ree) receptors—sensory structures that detect pheromones and other kinds of odors. Olfactory receptors are located in different places in the bodies of different kinds of animals.

pheromones (FEHR-uh-mohns)—chemicals, or mixtures of chemicals, that are produced and released by one animal and that bring about a specific response in other animals of the same species

pores—small holes in the olfactory receptors located on the antennae of invertebrates, through which pheromone molecules enter

pupa (PEW-puh)—the third stage in the development of honey bees and other insects, during which the body of the adult insect is formed. Plural, **pupae (PEW-pee).**

queen bee—a large female bee that normally lays all the eggs in a honey bee colony. Pheromone messages sent by the queen control many activities within the colony.

queen cells—large, acorn-shaped cells in which young queen bees develop

queen substance—one of the pheromones produced by the mandibular (jaw) glands of queen bees

recognition pheromones—chemical messages that help animals to recognize their homes or other members of their own species

scent brushes—specialized organs used by some kinds of male butterflies to disperse pheromones. Scent brushes (also known as **hair pencils**) are covered with fine hairs that make it possible for the chemicals to evaporate rapidly.

scent mark—a chemical message left when pheromones are deposited on the ground, on objects, or on other animals

sex pheromones—chemical messages that bring male and female animals of the same species together for mating

stimuli (STIM-yuh-lie)—actions or situations that can bring about a reaction in living things. The singular form of the word is **stimulus.**

swarming—the process by which a honey bee colony divides and forms a new colony

trail pheromones—chemical messages released into the air or deposited on surfaces to form a trail that can be followed by other animals of the same species

worker bees—female bees that do all the work in a honey bee colony. The particuar job that a worker performs depends on her age.

INDEX

aggregation pheromones, 21
alarm pheromones, 23, 26; of honey
    bees, 43-44
antennae, 19, 21
ants, 14, 24, 26
aphids, 23-24
apple maggot fly, 22-23

bark beetles, 21-22
beaver, pheromones of, 28
black-tailed deer, 26-27
bombykol, 13-14, 21, 28
Butenandt, Adolf, 13
butterflies, use of pheromones by, 16

cats, use of pheromones by, 18
cells (in bee nest), 33
chemical communication (other than
    pheromones), 10-11
combs of bee nest, 32-33
court of queen bee, 46

dance, bee, 40, 45; used during swarming,
    51, 53, 55
deer, use of pheromones by, 14, 17, 26-27
dispersal pheromones, 22-23
dogs, use of pheromones by, 10, 18, 21
drones, 35-36, 45, 48

eggs of honey bees, 31, 32, 36, 50

fireflies, communication of, 7, 9-10
fish, 19, 23
footprint pheromones of queen bee, 49
foragers, 35, 45

glands, pheromone, 10, 14, 16, 26, 27; of
    honey bees, 42, 43, 46

guard bees, 43

hair pencils, 16
Hecker, Erich, 13
honey, 35, 36, 43
human pheromones, 59

insecticides, 58
insects, use of pheromones by, 13, 28.
    See also individual insects.

larva of honey bee, 36, 38, 45, 50
lemurs, 25-26

mammals, use of pheromones by, 28
mandibular gland pheromones, 46
moths, use of pheromones by, 13-14, 16, 19, 21

Nasonov pheromone, 43, 51-52, 53, 55;
    used to attract pollinators, 57
Nasonov scent gland, 43
nectar, 35
nurse bees, 32, 45

olfactory receptors, 19, 21

pests, insects, pheromones used to
    control, 58-59
pollen, 35, 36
pollinators, insects as, 57
pores, 19, 21
predators, 11
pupa of honey bee, 38, 45

queen bee, 31, 32, 36; development of,
    50, 51, 53; as egg-layer, 31, 36, 48, 49,
    50; pheromones of, 45-46, 48, 49, 50,
    51, 55; role of, in swarming, 49-55

queen cells, 33, 49-50
queen substance, 46, 48

rabbits, use of pheromones by, 7, 10, 17-18
recognition pheromones, 26-27
research on pheromones, 13, 14, 27-29, 57, 58, 59
royal jelly, 36, 50

scent brushes, 16
scent marks, 17-18
scout bees, 50-51, 53, 55
sex pheromones, 13-14, 21; used against insect pests, 58
silkworm moths, 13-14
skunks, chemical communication of, 10-11
social insects, 31
sounds as means of communication, 7, 9
spiders, 21

stimuli causing pheromone release, 16
stings, bee, 43-44
swarming, 48-55; causes of, 48, 49, 50; role of queen in, 49, 51, 55
synthetic pheromones, 57

tarsal glands, 27
termites, 24
trail pheromones, 26; of honey bees, 45
traps baited with pheromones, 58-59

visual signals as means of communication, 7, 9-10

wax, 32
wolves, use of pheromones by, 18
worker bees, 36, 40, 48, 49-50, 51; jobs of, in colony, 32-33, 35, 45-46; use of pheromones by, 43-44, 51-52, 53, 55

ACKNOWLEDGMENTS The photographs and drawings in this book are reproduced through the courtesy of: p. 6, Colin Photographics© 1989; p. 7, Minneapolis Public Library and Information Center; p. 8, Satoshi Kuribayashi; p. 11, Independent Picture Service; pp. 12, 15 (bottom), Isao Kishida; pp. 15 (top), 27, D. Muller-Schwarze; p. 17 (top), Thomas Eisner; p. 17 (bottom), Martin C. Birch; p. 18, Scot Stewart; p. 19, Dwight R. Kuhn; pp. 20, 56, 58, 59, Agricultural Research Service, USDA; p. 22, ESA/Ries Memorial Slide Collection; p. 23, New York State Experiment Station, Cornell University; p. 24, Dr. R. L. Nault, Ohio State University; p. 25, Alton Halverson; p. 29, Tom Seeley; pp. 30, 33, 35, 37, 38, 39, 41, 43, 44, 47, 49, 52, 54, Kenneth Lorenzen, University of California, Davis; pp. 32, 34, 42, 50, Rebecca L. Johnson; p. 36, Dr. Basil Furgala, University of Minnesota.